YouTube Script Writing

The Content Creator's Guide to Crafting Entertaining, Informative, and Captivating Scripts for Viral Videos

Preface

Everybody knows that the secret sauce for an awesome YouTube channel is having a killer script! You might have the coolest video editor on the planet, your camera quality could be out of this world, heck, you could splurge on all sorts of gadgets and set up the fanciest studio with dazzling lights and backgrounds. But, truth bomb: if your script isn't packing the right punch to hook people in, your video won't be the next big thing.

We've all heard those exclamations like "OMG! It was crazy, absolutely mind-blowing; I just couldn't stop watching!" Bet you've come across a bunch of those. And what about this classic line, ever heard it? "So, I stumbled upon this video on YouTube." Now, let me throw a question your way. How do you reckon people stumble onto a video? Were they on a mission to find that particular video, or did it just pop up, impossible to resist, making them hit play and invest some serious time?

Over time, you'll notice that a lot of subscribers aren't actively hunting for a specific video. Nope, they usually trip over a video and then decide it's worth their while. Like, "I was supposed to be looking for study materials on YouTube for my exam tomorrow, but then I found this video, and I just couldn't look away!"

And you can bet your last dollar that when this person heads back to YouTube, they're going to be on the lookout for new videos from that channel, hungry for more content. That right there is the magic of a top-notch script – it doesn't just grab attention; it hooks people in for the long haul, turning casual viewers into avid fans waiting for the next big thing!

What's Inside

Hit me with the Juice!

In the not-so-distant past, the idea of surfing through countless videos on the internet, hoping to find something captivating, was an alien concept. Back in the early days of YouTube, users would visit the platform with a specific video in mind, a destination carefully chosen before boarding on their digital expedition. It was a time when YouTube was a repository of specific content rather than the boundless sea of possibilities it is today.

YouTube, born in 2005, was a humble platform designed for users to share and watch videos. The landscape was simple, and the choices were limited. Users would type precise keywords, hoping to stumble upon the exact content they craved. It was a time when the platform was akin to a video library, with users as diligent curators, carefully selecting each piece of content to consume.

However, the digital ecosystem evolves at a breathtaking pace, and YouTube is no exception. As more creators flocked to the platform, a content bloom erupted. Suddenly, YouTube wasn't just a place for planned visits; it transformed into a bustling marketplace of ideas, creativity, and entertainment. The platform's algorithm, once a rudimentary guide, became a sophisticated curator, capable of understanding user preferences and predicting what might capture their attention.

In the early days, users navigated YouTube with intent. They had a specific video or content genre in mind, and the search bar was their gateway. Fast forward a couple of years, and the landscape has changed dramatically. The sheer volume of content demanded a new approach to exploration. Users found themselves drifting through the vast ocean of videos, guided not by a predetermined destination but by the promise of surprise and novelty.

The shift from a destination-oriented platform to one of discovery was fueled by a fundamental change in user behavior. People were no longer content with simply seeking out what they knew they liked. Instead, they began to trust YouTube's algorithm to serve up a diverse array of content, much like a personal concierge for digital entertainment.

The phrase "Hit me with the juice" has become emblematic of this shift in user behavior. It encapsulates the idea that users now approach YouTube with a sense of openness, relinquishing control to the algorithmic wizardry that underpins the platform. But how does YouTube decide what "the juice" is for each individual? So, what is the YouTube algorithm all about, and how does it work?

YouTube's algorithm takes into account your watch history and search queries. If you've been binging on tech reviews or cooking tutorials, the algorithm notes your preferences. YouTube employs machine learning and predictive analysis to understand patterns in user behavior. It learns from your interactions with the platform to anticipate what might capture your interest next. Engagement metrics, such as likes, comments, and shares, play a crucial role. If a video resonates with a particular audience segment, the algorithm is likely to recommend it to similar users. YouTube's algorithm assesses the relevance of a video to your interests. This involves analyzing video titles, descriptions, and tags to ensure the content aligns with your preferences.

The amount of time you spend watching a video or a series of videos influences the algorithm's suggestions. If a video keeps you glued to the screen, YouTube sees it as a positive signal.

PewDiePie, one of YouTube's most subscribed creators, is a case in point. Over the years, his content has evolved from gaming to a broader range of entertainment. The algorithm recognized this shift and adapted recommendations accordingly, introducing viewers to PewDiePie's diverse content offerings.

YouTube also uses a Genre-hopping system called "Recommended for you" This is usually completely different from what you would normally go for, but the algorithm is trying to figure out what else you are interested in so that it can suggest more videos to you. Remember, YouTube aims to "keep you here as long as possible" In darker terms, we would refer to it as "Take your soul and keep you here, watching videos, forever!" here's how Genre-hopping works, Consider a user who primarily watches travel vlogs. YouTube's algorithm might surprise them with a video from a completely different genre, like a science documentary or a cooking tutorial. This cross-genre recommendation strategy aims to broaden users' horizons and introduce them to new interests.

YouTube's trending page is a testament to the algorithm's ability to identify videos on the verge of virality. A video's rapid rise in views, combined with other engagement metrics, can propel it to the coveted trending section, exposing it to a wider audience.

As a content creator, understanding the convolutions of YouTube's algorithm is to stand out in this vast digital landscape. Crafting scripts that not only resonate with your audience but also align with the platform's recommendation mechanisms can elevate your content from the depths of obscurity to the shores of popularity. As obvious as they may seem, let's look at some of the key strategies to scripting successful content:

Understanding your target audience is the first step. Tailor your content to their interests, addressing topics that resonate with them.

YouTube's algorithm pays attention to how long viewers watch a video. Captivate your audience from the start with engaging introductions to increase retention.

Craft titles and descriptions that accurately represent your content and include relevant keywords. This helps the algorithm understand the context of your video.

Likes, comments, and shares signal to the algorithm that your content is engaging. Encourage viewers to interact with your videos to boost visibility.

Regular uploads create a sense of consistency, encouraging viewers to return for more. The algorithm recognizes this and may reward your channel with increased visibility.

The days of meticulously planning your digital viewing are long gone, replaced by the thrill of unpredictability and the magic of algorithmic curation. So, let's explore the art of crafting compelling narratives, leveraging humor, and mastering the fine balance between education and entertainment.

One thing that big channels never talk about is their script. You should know that their script is the ultimate weapon and everything else is the distraction that takes you away from the true money maker itself—the brilliant script. But when you look past aesthetics, you will realize that the cohesive force that binds all the elements together into a chasm of entertainment is the script. I call it, the "Genjutsu"

Word Genjutsu

In the massive expanse of YouTube, where attention is the most precious currency, the power of a well-crafted script cannot be negotiated. Like a skilled Shinobi employing Genjutsu to entrance their opponent, a brilliant script has the ability to weave a spell, captivating the viewer's mind, body, and soul.

Genjutsu is the art of creating an illusion so powerful that it ensnares the viewer in a state of captivation. It goes beyond mere words on a screen; it's about crafting an experience that elicits a profound emotional response. To comprehend the impact of Word Genjutsu, let's break down the key elements that contribute to this mesmerizing effect.

1. Emotional Manipulation:

The Word Genjutsu begins with a deep understanding of human emotions. A well-crafted script taps into the reservoir of feelings, guiding the viewer through a rollercoaster of highs and lows. Whether it's laughter, surprise, awe, or empathy, the script is a conductor orchestrating the emotional symphony.

Example:

In a travel vlog, the script doesn't just narrate the scenic beauty; it immerses the viewer in the awe-inspiring landscapes, evoking a sense of wanderlust. A sudden twist in the narrative, perhaps encountering unexpected challenges, triggers empathy and suspense, keeping the viewer on the edge of their seat.

2. Tapping into Nerves:

Word Genjutsu extends its influence to the physical realm, tapping into the viewer's nerves. A carefully chosen word, a dramatic pause, or a sudden change in tone can send shivers down the spine or induce a burst of adrenaline. The script becomes a tactile experience, making the viewer's nerves dance to its rhythm.

Example:

In a horror-themed video, the script doesn't rely solely on visual elements. Instead, it uses words to describe the eerie silence, the creaking floorboards, and the subtle whispers, creating an atmosphere that reaches beyond the screen and infiltrates the viewer's senses.

3. The Loop of Addiction:

Word Genjutsu, at its core, is about creating an addiction loop. A captivating script doesn't just end; it leaves the viewer craving more. Each video becomes a stepping stone, seamlessly connecting to the next, creating a narrative flow that is irresistible.

Example:

A gaming channel doesn't conclude an episode abruptly. Instead, the script plants seeds of curiosity, hinting at future challenges, story developments, or unexpected twists. Viewers, now entrapped in the narrative, eagerly anticipate the next installment, unable to break free from the addiction loop.

While Word Genjutsu forms the core of captivating scripts, it's essential to expand our arsenal of techniques. Let's explore additional concepts that, when combined with Word Genjutsu, create a potent formula for scripting success.

1. The Visual Symphony:

A script is not confined to words alone; it's a visual symphony that engages the viewer on multiple levels. Descriptive language, vivid imagery, and well-timed visual cues enhance the viewing experience, making it a feast for the eyes.

Example:

A cooking tutorial doesn't merely list ingredients and steps; the script paints a picture of colors, textures, and aromas. It describes the sizzle of ingredients in the pan, the vibrant hues of fresh produce, and the irresistible aroma wafting through the kitchen, engaging the viewer's senses beyond taste.

2. The Echoing Motif:

A recurring motif in a script acts as a psychological anchor, embedding itself in the viewer's memory. Whether it's a catchphrase, a visual element, or a thematic thread, the motif creates a sense of familiarity, fostering a connection that goes beyond individual videos.

Example:

A beauty vlogger consistently uses a signature background music track in their videos. Over time, viewers associate this tune with the vlogger's content. When they hear it elsewhere, it triggers an automatic connection, leading them back to the familiar world of the channel.

3. Interactive Engagement:

Break down the barrier between creator and viewer by incorporating interactive elements. Encourage comments, pose questions, and create opportunities for viewers to actively participate. This transforms the viewing experience from passive consumption to an immersive, two-way dialogue.

Example:

A science channel ends each video with a thought-provoking question, prompting viewers to share their opinions in the comments. The script not only imparts knowledge but also invites viewers to contribute to the ongoing conversation, fostering a sense of community and engagement.

4. The Surprise Element:

Keep viewers on their toes by injecting an element of surprise. Whether it's an unexpected twist in the narrative, a sudden change in tone, or a surprising revelation, the script becomes a vehicle for unpredictability, preventing content from becoming predictable or monotonous.

Example:

A comedy skit takes an unexpected turn, subverting the viewer's expectations. The script, through its clever use of comedic timing and unconventional punchlines, keeps the audience guessing and eagerly awaiting the next surprise.

The ultimate goal of Genjutsu-infused scripting is to cast a spell so potent that viewers willingly succumb to its influence. The loop of addiction tightens, and a casual viewer transforms into a devoted subscriber.

Consistency is Key

Just as a ninja hones their skills through rigorous training, consistency in content is the cornerstone of building a subscriber base. Regular uploads, a consistent tone, and a cohesive brand identity create an expectation that keeps viewers coming back for more. For Instance, a lifestyle vlogger consistently shares snippets of their daily routine, maintaining a predictable upload schedule. Viewers, accustomed to this rhythm, integrate the vlogger's content into their daily routine, establishing a sense of familiarity and reliance.

YouTube is dynamic, and successful creators adapt to changing trends. The script, too, must evolve. Pay attention to audience feedback, stay attuned to industry shifts, and be willing to experiment. This adaptability ensures that your content remains relevant and continues to captivate. For instance, a tech review channel, originally focused on smartphones, adapts to emerging trends by incorporating coverage of cutting-edge gadgets and innovations. The script, reflecting this evolution, becomes a narrative of technological progress, resonating with both loyal subscribers and new viewers.

Youtube Scriptwriting Vs. Conventional Scriptwriting

If you are new to Youtube script writing then you may be wondering, what is the difference between a youtube script and a play or movie script? You may even have the wrong idea of what the scripts looks like. Here's an example:

Title: "The Haunting Shadows"

Setting: A dimly lit, old Victorian house. The only source of light is a flickering lamp on a dusty table

---

Scene 1: Living Room, Night

The room is shrouded in darkness. JESSICA nervously enters, glancing around.

JESSICA: (muttering to herself) This place gives me the creeps.

The lamp flickers, casting eerie shadows on the walls.

MR. COLLINS: (appearing suddenly) Welcome, Jessica. I trust you'll find everything to your liking.

JESSICA: (nervously) Yeah, it's... charming.

MR. COLLINS chuckles, his eyes glinting mysteriously.

Scene 2: Bedroom, Later

JESSICA lies in bed, trying to sleep. Strange noises echo through the house.

JESSICA: (whispering) Just my imagination... just my imagination.

The shadows seem to dance on the walls. Suddenly, a sinister figure, THE SHADOW, emerges.

THE SHADOW: (whispering) Jessica...

JESSICA gasps, frozen in terror.

Scene 3: Living Room, Next Morning

JESSICA confronts MR. COLLINS.

JESSICA: There's something in this house, Mr. Collins. I saw it!

MR. COLLINS: (smirking) Ah, the shadows have taken a liking to you.

JESSICA: I want out of this place. Now!

MR. COLLINS reveals a sinister grin as the shadows seem to envelop the room.JESSICA desperately tries to leave, but the door won't budge.

JESSICA: (panicking) What is happening?

MR. COLLINS: (chanting) You've awakened the shadows, Jessica. They won't let you go.

THE SHADOW appears, growing larger and more menacing.

THE SHADOW: (whispering) You're ours now.

The room descends into darkness as chilling laughter echoes.

Curtain Falls

This is what you are probably more familiar with, but no, that was a play script which of course can be developed into a movie script. A Youtube script is more like this:

Geography Channel

Something Incredible has emerged at the Grand Canyon...

An unexplained phenomenon has unfolded right before our very eyes! The Grand Canyon has given birth to an awe-inspiring enigma that has defied scientific explanation and human logic. Scientists are completely dazed at how something so profound can exist in the Grand Canyon for this long a time, and finally its mysteries has been brought to light.

As the old saying goes, some truths are better off left buried. Places such as the Grand Canyon have always been controversial, to the extent that it is considered as one of the 7 wonders of the world, but nothing will prepare you for the mystery that this historical place holds and what it has brought to the surface. Get ready for an astonishing discovery that has left experts speechless!

Welcome to the captivating world of geographical mysteries, where we explore the mysterious and unexplained happenings that unveil the metaphysical.

From breathtaking landscapes to geological wonders, the Grand Canyon has always fascinated explorers and scientists alike. But what we have stumbled upon goes beyond anything we could have imagined. In this thrilling investigation, we will reveal a 5000 year old technology that has captivated the attention of experts from around the world and got the world asking—are we safe? And most importantly, what does this mean for mankind.

Stay with us till the end of the video, as we unearth the mystery of the 5000 year old tech, piece by piece, and reveal the astounding truth behind this mind-boggling discovery. You won't want to miss a single moment of this captivating expedition to uncover the secrets that lie beneath the majestic cliffs of the Grand Canyon.

Can We Reverse Aging?

Humans, for the longest time, have told stories of demi gods, immortals, and mythical creatures who have transcended mortality, possessing the gift of long life, could these stories have emanated from the desire of humans to overcome their biggest limitation—aging?

Is there a way for humans to reverse aging? It's a question that has fascinated scientists and sparked the imagination of people for centuries. We all know that aging is an inevitable part of the human life, but could there be a way to turn back the clock and revitalize our bodies to stay young for years to come?

To understand the possibility of reversing aging, we need to explore the complicated world of the human body, starting with the smallest unit of life—our cells. At the core of our being lies our DNA, the blueprint of life. As we grow and become of age, our cells divide and replicate, with our DNA passed on to new cells. Over time, our cells, which contain telomeres, divide and replicate till we begin to age. How does this happen?

The telomeres at the ends of our chromosomes shorten during DNA replication but the enzyme telomerase replaces the fragment of telomeres that was lost or shortened during the DNA replication process. This sequence is repeated all through our youth until a point where the production of the enzyme telomerase reduces and then our telomeres are unable to replace themselves. Our telomeres become shorter and shorter with each DNA replication, causing the deterioration of our system, our organs become frail, our bodies do not get enough genetic materials to maintain our youth and we slowly begin to age physically, leading to incapacitation and eventually, cells die and as a result, so do we.

But what if we could find a way to halt or even reverse this process?

Let's take a look at the field of anti-aging research, where scientists are exploring various approaches to fight aging and extend our healthspan.

One promising avenue is the study of telomeres themselves. Researchers are investigating ways to lengthen telomeres artificially, potentially slowing down or even reversing the aging process. Telomerase, an enzyme that plays a significant role in synthesis of telomere and its maintenance, is a key focus of this research.

Another area of exploration in the field of regenerative medicine is the Stem cells. Imagine that the body is one big shopping mall and an injury occurs in one of the aisles, let's say a crate of eggs shatter to the floor, causing damage in the body. The human body begins a process of renewal and regrowth by sending a voice message to the stem cell that is the janitor and is located in the bone marrow. The stem cell drives a mobile cart to the injured area in the body and begins to clean up the aisle, and to replace the eggs that have been destroyed. The importance of this powerful janitor is that it has the super power to develop into different types of cells, and holds immense potential in rejuvenating aging tissues and organs. By harnessing the power of stem cells, scientists are aiming to restore youthful vitality to damaged or aged body parts.

Additionally, the study of senescence, which is a state of irreversible cell cycle arrest, has gained the attention of scientists. Cells typically fight to defend themselves from harm and when they are compromised they find a way to repair themselves. However, some cells may become compromised but still continue to replicate, creating new cells that are dangerous to the body. This is where Senescence becomes important. A senescent cell is one that has been damaged but not to critical level. The cell decides to go into a state of self-arrest, stopping itself from participating in cell replication or other activities. This self-isolation saves other cells around it from being compromised or infected, leaving only perfectly healthy cells to replicate. Senescent cells, which accumulate as we age, may become a bad thing when they are in excess. The inflammatory content emitted by the senescent cells to help other cells around them may become problematic around organs such as liver or heart that are already experiencing inflammation. Developing therapies to selectively remove or rejuvenate these cells could offer significant anti-aging benefits.

Beyond cellular interventions, researchers are also exploring the role of lifestyle factors in reversing the aging process. Caloric restriction, intermittent fasting, and regular exercises have shown promising effects in extending human lifespan and promoting overall health. These interventions influence cellular processes, metabolism, and the expression of genes related to aging.

While the research on reversing aging is still in its early stages, the future holds exciting possibilities. The pursuit of unlocking the secrets of longevity is driven by the desire to improve the quality of life for individuals and potentially address age-related diseases.

However, it's important to approach the topic with cautious optimism. Aging is an incredibly complex process influenced by numerous factors, and complete reversal may remain elusive. But as science advances and our understanding deepens, the dream of extending our healthspan and embracing a more vibrant future becomes increasingly within reach.

Can humans reverse aging? Only time will tell. But as we uncover the mysteries of our biology and push the boundaries of scientific knowledge, one thing is certain: the quest for a longer, healthier life is a journey worth embarking upon.

Lifestyle Channel

Andrew Tate's Luxury Supercar Collection

Andrew Tate has some of the most expensive Speed demons on the market. We call him Andrew "Taste" because his taste in luxury supercars is unmatched. I mean, Ferrari, Lamborghini, Rolls Royce, Aston Martin, Porsche, all these big names all reside in the controversial influencer's garage. You may not agree with what he says, but you will certainly approve of what he rides. One of the cars is so expensive that you need to be super rich to even afford to fuel the automotive apex predator. Stick with us to the end and we will not only tell you how expensive and fast these luxury sports cars are, but also how much CO_2 emissions they drop on us. It's no wonder global warming is out of control. Tate is killing the atmosphere for us out here.

Starting at number one, we have the Italian Superfast sports car, the Ferrari 812

This beautiful specimen packs a 789bhp and tears its way up to 211mph. The luxury ride barely does 12 miles per gallon and who could blame it with its speed ability. Now don't lose your cool, climate geeks, but this ride emits a shocking 340 grams of CO_2 per kilometer. If you think that's a problem then wait till you see the rest of the cars on the list. This car is so special, no wonder Tate likes to pose with it on Instagram. The Ferrari 812 costs 335,000 pounds.

Next on the list, we have the slick McLaren 720S

The twin-turbo V8 sports car is jaw-droppingly gorgeous and is no stranger to the race tracks. If you want a fast car that can go from zero to 120 mph in less than seven, this is certainly the one. It is slightly more green than some other supercars that Tate owns when it comes to its emissions, with 249 grams of CO_2 per kilometer. The McLaren is unique, portable, and reeks of affluence. The car costs as much as 255,000 pounds.

Imagine you're sitting down with your audience for a friendly chat. That's the essence of YouTube script writing. It's like the difference between a casual coffee date and a formal dinner party.

Informality Rules:

YouTube scripts are laid-back, almost like you're talking to a friend. No need for fancy words or complicated sentences. It's all about being authentic, showing your real self. Imagine you're explaining a concept to your buddy over pizza.

Bite-sized Brilliance:

Keep it short and sweet. YouTube audiences have a shorter attention span, so you want to grab their interest quickly and hold onto it. Think of it like telling a captivating story in the time it takes to finish a snack.

Visual Feast:

Since it's a visual platform, visuals and graphics are your best pals. You're not just telling a story; you're showing it. Use on-screen text, engaging visuals, and maybe even a dash of humor. It's like adding spices to a dish – you want it to be flavorful!

Instant Connection:

Here's the magic of YouTube – you get instant feedback. Comments, likes, and shares start pouring in as soon as your video goes live. It's like having a conversation with your audience in real-time. You say something, and they react immediately.

Monetization Game:

Making money on YouTube involves ads, sponsorships, and affiliate marketing. Your script needs to seamlessly incorporate these elements without feeling forced. Think of it like recommending your favorite products to a friend – genuine and unobtrusive.

Global Party:

Your YouTube script is an open invitation to a global party. People from different corners of the world can join in. It's like hosting a virtual gathering where everyone's welcome.

Traditional Scripting: Crafting Epics

Now, let's switch gears and imagine you're composing an epic tale for the big screen or the stage. It's a bit like preparing for a grand theatrical performance.

Structured Symphony:

Traditional scripts follow a specific structure – acts, scenes, dialogues. It's like composing a symphony with distinct movements. Your script is the sheet music, and everyone, from actors to directors, follows it to create a harmonious performance.

Character Symphony:

Characters are your orchestra. You're not just chatting; you're orchestrating the movements of each character to convey a larger-than-life story. Each character has a role, a purpose, and a journey to embark on. It's like conducting a symphony where every instrument has its part to play.

Visuals Through Dialogue:

Unlike YouTube, where visuals are right in front of your audience, in traditional scripts, you paint pictures with words.

The dialogue becomes the brush, creating vivid scenes and landscapes in the minds of the audience.

Delayed Gratification:

Feedback doesn't flood in immediately. You have to wait until the production is complete, and the audience experiences it. It's like planting a seed and patiently waiting for the tree to grow.

Business Backstage:

Monetization in the traditional realm comes from ticket sales, distribution deals, and contracts. The business side is handled behind the scenes. Your focus as a writer is on crafting an engaging narrative rather than worrying about product placements.

Local Premieres:

Unlike the global reach of YouTube, traditional scripts might have more localized premieres, especially in theaters. It's akin to hosting a grand opening night for a select audience.

Writing Techniques: Bridging the Worlds

Now that we've explored the distinct vibes of YouTube and traditional scripting, let's talk about some writing techniques that can bridge these two worlds.

Whether you're writing for YouTube or the big screen, the core is storytelling. Master the art of weaving a compelling narrative that captivates your audience. It's like being a master chef – the ingredients may vary, but the goal is to create a delightful dish. Characters are the heartbeat of any script. Whether you're introducing them in a YouTube video or a feature film, make them relatable and nuanced. Imagine your characters as old friends – you know them inside out, and your audience should feel the same.

Your dialogue is the bridge between you and your audience. It should be natural, impactful, and true to the tone of your script. It's like having a conversation with your audience, whether you're chatting casually on YouTube or presenting a profound dialogue in a play.

Even if you're writing for YouTube, don't neglect the power of words to create mental images. Similarly, in traditional scripts, let your visuals be vivid through expressive dialogue. It's like being a painter – whether you're using a canvas or a screen, your goal is to create a visual masterpiece.

 In the YouTube world, it's about maintaining a swift rhythm. In traditional scripts, it's about orchestrating the flow of the story.

Getting Started with Youtube Scriptwriting

The first thing to do is to Identify your niche and target audience. Knowing who you're creating content for will guide your scriptwriting style and content. Next, you must Familiarize yourself with basic script structures such as introductions, hooks, body content, and conclusions. YouTube scripts often follow a conversational and engaging format. This means analyze popular channels in your niche. Observe how they structure their scripts, engage with their audience, and maintain a consistent tone. Experiment with different styles until you find your unique voice. Whether it's humor, education, or storytelling, make sure it resonates with your audience. Grab your viewers' attention in the first few seconds. Create compelling hooks and introductions to encourage viewers to stay and watch the entire video.

While scripting, remember to encourage likes, comments, and subscriptions. Pose questions, ask for opinions, and create a sense of community within your audience. Clearly state what you want your viewers to do next. Whether it's subscribing, watching another video, or leaving a comment, include CTAs. Edit your script for clarity and conciseness. Ensure it flows naturally and maintains a conversational tone.

The final stage is to practice delivering your script, record yourself, and review the footage. Pay attention to pacing, tone, and overall presentation.

Building a Youtube Scriptwriting Portfolio

A well-curated portfolio not only demonstrates your expertise but also provides tangible evidence of your ability to create compelling and engaging content. The essence of building a portfolio is to give you credibility, especially when applying as script writer to big channels. Here's a step-by-step guide on how to build an impressive YouTube scriptwriting portfolio:

1. Create High-Quality Sample Scripts: Develop a set of sample scripts that showcase your versatility. Cover different genres, tones, and formats to demonstrate your adaptability. Aim for scripts that reflect the type of projects you want to attract.

2. Include Diverse Genres and Styles: Showcase a range of genres and writing styles in your portfolio. Include scripts for educational content, comedy sketches, informational videos, and any other genres that align with your interests and skills.

3. Write Spec Scripts for Existing Channels: Choose a few existing YouTube channels that you admire and create spec scripts for them. This not only demonstrates your understanding of their style but also shows your potential clients that you can seamlessly fit into different brand voices.

4. Craft Compelling Loglines and Summaries: Accompany each script with a compelling logline or summary. This provides a quick overview of the script's theme, tone, and intended impact. Make sure these summaries are concise and enticing.

5. Create a Professional Website or Portfolio Platform: Build a professional website or use portfolio platforms like Behance or Contently to showcase your work. Include an "About Me" section, your resume, and a dedicated section for your YouTube script samples.

6. **Develop a Personal Brand:**

Consider developing a personal brand that aligns with your niche or preferred writing style. This could include a consistent visual theme, logo, or tagline that sets you apart.

7. Include Testimonials and Recommendations: If you've worked with clients or collaborators in the past, include testimonials or recommendations in your portfolio. Positive feedback from others can build trust and credibility.

8. Demonstrate Results: Whenever possible, include metrics or results from your previous work. For instance, if a video script you wrote garnered a high number of views, engagement, or shares, highlight those statistics to showcase your impact.

9. Provide Links to Produced Content: If you've had the opportunity to see your scripts turned into actual videos, provide links to the produced content. This offers tangible proof of your ability to create scripts that translate into engaging videos.

10. Optimize for SEO: Optimize your portfolio for search engines by including relevant keywords in your content. This increases the likelihood of your portfolio being discovered by those searching for YouTube scriptwriters.

11. Highlight Your Unique Selling Proposition (USP): Clearly articulate what sets you apart as a scriptwriter. Whether it's a unique approach, a specific skill, or your ability to connect with diverse audiences, make your USP evident in your portfolio.

12. Keep it Updated: Regularly update your portfolio with new scripts, projects, or achievements. An updated portfolio not only reflects your current capabilities but also signals your commitment to your craft.

13. Network and Collaborate: Actively participate in the YouTube and content creator communities. Collaborate with other creators, showcase your scripts, and build a network that can vouch for your skills and potentially provide job opportunities.

14. Engage in Social Media: Utilize social media platforms to share snippets of your scripts, engage with discussions in the writing and content creation communities, and promote your portfolio.

15. Seek Feedback and Iterate: Encourage constructive feedback from peers, mentors, or even potential clients. Use this feedback to continuously improve your scripts and portfolio presentation.

16. Freelance Platforms and Job Boards: Explore freelance platforms like Upwork, Freelancer, or Fiverr, as well as job boards like Indeed or Glassdoor. These platforms can connect you with clients looking for scriptwriting services.

17. Pitch to YouTube Channels or Production Companies: Actively pitch your services to YouTube channels, production companies, or content creators in need of scriptwriters. Tailor your pitch to showcase how your skills align with their content needs.

18. Participate in Scriptwriting Contests: Enter scriptwriting contests or competitions. Winning or even participating in recognized competitions can add credibility to your portfolio.

19. Offer Free Workshops or Webinars: Host free workshops or webinars on YouTube scriptwriting. This not only positions you as an expert but also allows potential clients to experience your expertise firsthand.

Attraction + Attention = Money

A child is walking on the road, he spots a shiny object and goes "Oooooooh, what is that?" The child goes to explore this captivating object and right before he gets there he spots another shiny object that is a bit closer to him, once again, he goes "oooohhhh, what is that?" He changes destination and walks towards the second shiny object. On getting close, he realizes that he is surrounded by thousands of shiny objects which all potentially could be gold. The child is at a dilemma and wants to grab as many shiny objects as he can but his attention is greatly diverted as he is unable to stick to one task. This describes a category of viewers on youtube. This is called the **"Shiny object category"**

The second category of audience is called the **"Bread Crumb category"** Here's an illustration. A young girl is in the woods, exploring nature and sniffing beautiful flowers. She sees a crumb of bread on the ground. She picks it up and taste's it. The bread crumb appears to be the tastiest bread that she has ever tasted. She becomes anxious for more and just as she was about to lose hope, she spots another bread crumb. She sprints over to it and picks it up, and just then, something catches her eyes... a trail of bread crumbs in a straight line, leading deeper into the woods. She follows loyally, picking the bread crumbs and eating them, until she arrives at a rabbit hole. She says to herself " There's more in there, I can't stop now" the little girl dives head-first into the rabbit hole... I think you get the point by now.

The Shiny Object represents the initial hook, the visual and auditory elements that capture immediate attention. In a world where content competes for microseconds of a viewer's focus, the visual appeal becomes a critical component.

A beauty tutorial script not only describes makeup techniques but uses visually captivating shots, vibrant colors, and expert lighting to make each step a visual spectacle. The allure of the "shiny" visuals entices viewers to stop scrolling and dive straight into the content.

Beyond aesthetics, relatability serves as a powerful shiny object. Scripts that incorporate personal anecdotes, relatable scenarios, or culturally relevant references create an immediate connection with the audience.

A lifestyle vlog script might include a segment where the creator shares a humorous mishap while trying a new fitness trend. Viewers, finding the situation relatable, are drawn in not just by the visual appeal but by the shared human experience.

Riding the wave of current trends is another facet of the shiny object. Scripts that incorporate popular memes, challenges, or trending topics leverage the collective attention already present in the online space.

A comedy sketch script could incorporate a popular internet meme as a recurring element, instantly appealing to viewers who are familiar with the trend. This not only adds a shiny and familiar aspect but also positions the content within the ongoing online conversation.

Once the shiny object captures attention, the bread crumbs come into play. These are narrative hooks strategically placed throughout the script, guiding the viewer from one engaging moment to the next.

A travel vlog script doesn't merely showcase picturesque destinations but incorporates narrative hooks like local legends, historical anecdotes, or personal reflections. These hooks serve as breadcrumbs, leading the viewer through a storytelling journey rather than a mere visual display.

The art of anticipation is a powerful breadcrumb strategy. Scripts that include teasers or hints about upcoming content create a sense of anticipation, encouraging viewers to stay connected for future releases.

A mystery-solving series script might end with a cryptic clue or a suspenseful teaser for the next episode. Viewers, intrigued by the breadcrumb of unresolved mysteries, eagerly anticipate the next installment.

Demographic Dynamics: Shaping Content for All Audiences

The Shiny Object and Bread Crumbs Theory is versatile, adapting seamlessly to diverse human demographics. Let's look at how this concept caters to various audience segments, acknowledging the unique preferences and expectations of different demographics.

1. Generation Z:

Gen Z, characterized by a penchant for authenticity and social causes, is drawn to visually appealing content with a purpose. The shiny object for this demographic might include vibrant visuals and relatable content, while the breadcrumbs involve interactive elements and a clear call-to-action for social engagement or support for a cause.

A lifestyle channel catering to Gen Z might incorporate visually striking content, addressing social issues in an authentic and relatable manner. Interactive elements like polls or challenges further enhance the engagement.

2. Millennials:

Millennials, marked by a blend of nostalgia and a desire for meaningful content, are attracted to scripts that tap into shared experiences and incorporate elements of humor or sentimentality. The shiny object here might be relatable scenarios or references, while the breadcrumbs involve narrative hooks that unfold a story over multiple episodes.

A comedy series script for millennials could incorporate nostalgic references to pop culture while weaving a narrative that unfolds gradually. Viewers are drawn in by the shiny appeal of familiar elements and stay engaged through the breadcrumbs of an evolving storyline.

3. Baby Boomers:

Baby boomers, appreciating authenticity and content that offers practical value, are drawn to scripts that provide clear information or cater to their interests. The shiny object might involve visually accessible and well-structured content, while the breadcrumbs include practical tips, advice, or follow-up information.

A DIY home improvement channel script for baby boomers could present visually clear instructions and tips for common household projects. Breadcrumbs might include follow-up episodes that build on previous projects or address viewer-submitted questions.

The Power of Niche Storytelling:

While appealing to broad demographics is essential, the power of niche storytelling should not be underestimated. Crafting scripts that cater to specific interests or subcultures within larger demographics can create a dedicated and engaged audience.

A food channel might specialize in a niche, such as vegan comfort food. The shiny object could be visually appealing recipes, and the breadcrumbs might involve exploring the cultural and ethical aspects of vegan cuisine, creating a narrative unique to the niche.

Emotional Arcs and Character Development:

Borrowing from traditional storytelling, incorporating emotional arcs and character development into scripts adds depth and resonance. Viewers become emotionally invested, and the combination of shiny objects (emotional highs) and breadcrumbs (character progression) keeps them hooked.

A scripted drama series on a channel could introduce characters with relatable struggles, and the shiny object might involve emotionally charged scenes. Breadcrumbs would be the gradual development of characters, making viewers eager to see how their stories unfold.

Youtube Script Writer's Dilemma

YouTube scriptwriters face several challenges when writing for various channels. These challenges can vary depending on the niche, audience, and content format, but some common issues include:

Audience Engagement

Who is my target audience?

How do I communicate in a language they understand?

What are their interests and inclinations?

What problems am I solving?

How do my audiences perceive my information?

How do I keep them engaged?

Keeping viewers engaged is the most important task of all for a script writer. Writers would have to dig deeper in creating content that captures and maintains the audience's interest from start to finish.

SEO Optimization

How do I optimize my script with keywords?

What keywords are my audiences searching for?

What terms are mostly used to find the sort of videos that I make?

With the vast amount of content on YouTube, getting videos discovered can be challenging. Writers need to incorporate relevant keywords, titles, and descriptions to optimize search engine visibility.

Content Variety

How diverse are my content?

What resonates more with my subscribers?

What videos are doing better than every other ones?

Depending on the channel, writers may need to balance the need for diverse content while maintaining a consistent brand identity. This can be challenging, especially if the audience has diverse interests.

Trends and Timeliness

What content is currently trending?

Is the trend popular with my target audience?

How long will it take to produce a video to meet the trending timeline?

Is the trend growing or is it in its depreciation phase?

Staying current with trends and creating timely content is essential. YouTube is a platform where trends come and go quickly, so writers must adapt to changing audience preferences.

Script Length

How long should my script be?

Does my script have enough information and entertainment to be lengthy?

What length of scripts provide the most desirable results?

Balancing the length of the script is crucial. Too short, and the content may lack depth; too long, and viewers might lose interest. Finding the right balance for the specific channel and audience is essential. Typically, videos around 8 to 20 minutes are desirable. This means scripts within 1000 to 4000 words.

Visual Engagement

What visuals will elevate my script?

How do I improve aesthetics and transitions on my videos?

YouTube is a visual platform, and writers need to create scripts that complement the visuals. This may involve coordinating with editors, incorporating graphics, and ensuring that the script translates well into a visually appealing video.

Adaptation to Algorithms

How does the algorithm work?

How do I write scripts that will be favored by the algorithm on longterm?

YouTube algorithms play a significant role in video visibility. Writers need to understand algorithmic preferences and tailor their scripts to align with platform requirements for higher visibility and engagement.

Community Interaction

How do I maintain close interaction with my community?

How do I sustain the support of my community?

How do I engage my community to keep their attention?

Engaging with the audience through comments and community features is essential for building a loyal following. Writers may need to consider this interaction when planning content and responding to feedback.

Script Originality

How do I keep my ideas fresh?

How do I continuously deliver unconventional ideas?

How do I avoid plagiarism and similar content?

Creating original content that stands out in a sea of videos is challenging. Writers need to find unique angles, perspectives, or formats to set their content apart from others in the same niche.

Monetization and Sponsorship Integration

How do I achieve my target in the shortest time possible?

How do I meet monetization requirement?

What other avenues can I make money through my channel?

For channels focused on monetization, writers may need to seamlessly integrate advertisements and sponsorships without compromising the overall quality and authenticity of the content.

Script Adaptation for Various Platforms

How do I make my content sharable on various other platforms?

Does my content also meet the standards and requirements of other platforms?

While YouTube may be the primary platform, scripts may also need adaptation for other social media platforms where the content is shared. Each platform has its own nuances and requirements.

Legal and Ethical Considerations:

Is my content offensive to any particular group?

Does it contain adult content or obscene stuff?

Is the language and ideology in line with guidelines?

Ensuring that the script adheres to copyright laws, community guidelines, and ethical standards is essential. This includes avoiding content that may be considered offensive or inappropriate.

The Relationship Between Script and visibility

Search Engine Optimization (SEO) is the gateway to visibility on YouTube. A strategically written script incorporates relevant keywords and phrases naturally, enhancing the video's discoverability. The script serves as the foundation upon which the algorithm builds connections between content and user queries.

A cooking tutorial script for a vegan lasagna not only describes the cooking process but strategically includes keywords like "vegan lasagna recipe," "plant-based lasagna," and "healthy vegan dinner ideas." This optimization ensures that the video is more likely to surface when users search for these terms.

The script dictates the essence of the video, shaping the creation of compelling thumbnails and titles. A well-crafted script ensures that the visual and textual elements align seamlessly, enticing viewers to click. This alignment enhances the click-through rate (CTR), a crucial metric for YouTube visibility.

A travel vlog script might detail a journey to a hidden paradise. The script inspires the creation of a thumbnail featuring the picturesque destination, coupled with a title like "Discovering Hidden Paradise: A Journey into Serenity." The script ensures that the video's content matches the promise made by the thumbnail and title, reducing the likelihood of viewer dissatisfaction.

When you think you don't need a script, that's when you need one

The misconception that some YouTube channels can thrive without a script often overlooks the strategic role scripting plays in creating engaging, focused, and successful content. It is referred to as **"The Illusion of Effortless Conversations"**

Many successful YouTube channels, especially those centered around vlogs, lifestyle, and casual conversations, may give the illusion of spontaneity. Creators effortlessly engage with their audience, sharing stories, thoughts, and experiences in a seemingly unscripted manner. The notion of using a script might seem counterintuitive to some. Yet, a closer look reveals that the most engaging and seemingly unscripted videos often owe their charm to a meticulously crafted script. We'll examine why even seemingly off-the-cuff YouTube channels benefit from scripts, the evidence of widespread script use, and the reasons YouTubers should consider scripting as an essential tool in their content creation arsenal.

Casey Neistat, a renowned vlogger, is known for his dynamic and seemingly spontaneous videos. However, he has mentioned in interviews that he carefully plans and scripts certain segments to ensure they convey the desired message effectively.

Vsauce, a popular educational channel, is known for its in-depth explorations of various topics. The host, Michael Stevens, uses scripted content to convey complex information in a way that is both entertaining and easy to follow.

H3H3 Productions, a channel known for its reaction videos and comedic commentary, often prepares scripted segments within their videos to ensure humor and commentary are well-crafted.

Linus Tech Tips, a channel focused on tech reviews and tutorials, scripts its content to ensure that complex information is communicated effectively. This attention to detail contributes to higher viewer engagement and better visibility within the tech community on YouTube.

Here are a few reasons why you should work with a script no matter how articulate you may be:

- Scripts provide a framework for delivering a clear and concise message. This is particularly important when conveying complex information, ensuring that viewers understand and retain the content. Without a script, creators might struggle with articulating their thoughts, leading to ambiguity or a lack of clarity in the video's message.
- Scripting streamlines the video production process, allowing creators to plan their shots, transitions, and visual elements efficiently. A script acts as a blueprint,

reducing the need for extensive editing or reshooting during the post-production phase.

- A well-scripted video is more likely to maintain viewer engagement throughout its duration, contributing to longer watch times and increased interaction. Unscripted content might lead to rambling or off-topic discussions that can result in viewer disinterest and a decline in engagement.

- Scripting ensures brand consistency across a creator's content. Whether it's the tone, style, or messaging, a script helps maintain a cohesive brand identity. Without a script, creators risk inconsistency, which can confuse viewers and dilute the overall brand image.

Which is more important, Video Editing, Script, or Thumbnail?

YouTube has evolved from being a platform for quirky cat videos to a global stage for content creators, educators, entertainers, and businesses to reach a massive audience. But what's the secret recipe for YouTube success? In this comprehensive exploration, we will analyze the trinity of elements that make up a successful YouTube channel: video editing, scriptwriting, and thumbnails. And, while each of these aspects plays a significant role, we'll try to make a compelling case for why scripting is the heart and soul of YouTube content.

The Trifecta of YouTube Success

Video Editing: This refers to the process of polishing raw footage, adding effects, transitions, and making the video visually appealing. Good video editing enhances the viewing experience, making it more engaging and professional.

Scriptwriting: Scripting is the art of crafting the spoken content of a video. A well-written script provides structure, clarity, and a compelling narrative that keeps viewers engaged and informed.

Thumbnails: Thumbnails are the small, clickable images that represent your video on YouTube. They serve as the first impression of your content and are crucial for attracting viewers' attention.

Now, let's take a closer look at the role of each element and how they interconnect in the grand scheme of YouTube success.

YouTube Channels and Their Success Stories

Vsauce

Michael Stevens, the creator of Vsauce, is widely recognized for his captivating educational content. While Vsauce's video editing and thumbnails are undoubtedly impressive, it's the quality of his scripting that sets his channel apart. Vsauce focuses on explaining complex scientific concepts with clarity and humor, and this is a testament to the power of a well-crafted script.

Vsauce videos often feature deep dives into scientific phenomena, puzzles, and brain teasers. The content could easily become overwhelming if not presented in an organized and engaging manner. The script is what ensures that viewers not only understand but also enjoy the content. The narrative structure, the pacing, and the explanations all stem from the script, making it the foundation of their videos.

TED-Ed

TED-Ed is known for its educational animations that are not only visually stunning but also intellectually stimulating. While their thumbnails are eye-catching, what truly sets their content apart is the exceptional scriptwriting. These well-researched, insightful scripts are the cornerstone of their educational videos, making them informative and engaging.

Consider a TED-Ed video on a complex historical event or a scientific theory. The script is what condenses the information into a digestible format, delivering knowledge in a way that captures the viewer's attention. Without a well-structured script, the stunning visuals and catchy thumbnails would lose their effectiveness in conveying the educational message.

CGP Grey

CGP Grey, known for his minimalist animations and simple thumbnails, proves that extravagant visuals are not a prerequisite for YouTube success. It's the meticulous scripting that keeps his audience engaged. CGP Grey's channel primarily focuses on explaining political, geographical, and historical topics. These are subjects that can easily turn dry and uninteresting, but his scripting brings life and clarity to these topics.

The scripting in CGP Grey's videos breaks down complex subjects with precision and an engaging narrative. The choice of words, the pacing, and the logical flow are all elements that stem from the script. Viewers often praise the clarity of his explanations, and this clarity is a direct result of the well-crafted scripts that underpin his content.

Why Scripting Takes the Crown

Now that we've explored some successful YouTube channels, it's time to dissect why scripting is often considered the most critical element in achieving YouTube success.

Content is King: Consider this: if the script is weak, no amount of fancy editing or eye-catching thumbnails can salvage the content. But a strong script can elevate even modest editing and thumbnails.

Engagement: A good script keeps your viewers engaged, informed, and entertained. YouTube is a highly competitive platform, and viewers have countless options. To capture and retain their attention, you need content that is not just visually appealing but also intellectually stimulating. A well-crafted script provides the foundation for such content.

SEO and Discoverability: Search Engine Optimization (SEO) is crucial for your content's discoverability on YouTube. Scripting plays a vital role in this. A well-structured script naturally incorporates keywords and phrases that improve your video's SEO. When people search for related topics, your video is more likely to appear in search results. Thus, scripting is essential for driving organic traffic to your channel.

Consistency: A script ensures consistency in your content, maintaining your channel's unique style and voice. Consistency is key to building a dedicated subscriber base. When viewers know what to expect from your channel, they are more likely to subscribe and return for more. This reliability stems from a well-structured script that maintains the same tone, style, and quality across videos.

Memorability: A great script can make your content memorable. Viewers are more likely to remember what you said and return for more. This memorability is essential for building a loyal audience. Whether it's a catchy catchphrase, a thought-provoking concept, or a heartfelt story, scripting plays a pivotal role in creating memorable moments in your videos.

Critical Examination of Video Editing and Thumbnails

While we've been emphasizing the importance of scripting, it's crucial to acknowledge that video editing and thumbnails are not to be underestimated. They play vital roles in attracting and retaining viewers. Let's take a closer look at their significance and how they complement scripting.

The Role of Video Editing:

Good video editing enhances the viewing experience. It's responsible for the pacing of your video, the smooth transitions between scenes, and the incorporation of visual effects that make the content engaging. A well-edited video can hold the viewer's attention, even if the scripting is strong. On the flip side, poor editing can detract from the overall quality of the content.

Video editing is especially crucial for channels that rely heavily on visual storytelling. Gaming channels, vlogs, and DIY channels often prioritize editing because it's an integral part of their content. However, even in these cases, the scripting is what guides the content, determines the story, and ensures that the message is clear and engaging.

The Significance of Thumbnails:

Thumbnails are the first impression of your video. They are like the book cover that potential readers judge before deciding to dive in. Thumbnails serve the purpose of attracting viewers' attention and enticing them to click on your video. An eye-catching thumbnail can significantly increase the click-through rate (CTR) of your videos.

Thumbnails are particularly important for new or lesser-known channels trying to break through the noise and establish a presence on YouTube. However, even the most enticing thumbnail won't lead to long-term success if the content doesn't deliver what it promises. It's in the content, driven by the script, that viewers find the substance they were looking for.

To drive home the point about the importance of thumbnails, consider this: while a compelling thumbnail can get viewers to click, it's the content that keeps them watching, engages them, and convinces them to subscribe. Thumbnails can lure viewers, but scripting is what ultimately retains and converts them into loyal subscribers.

So, if you're considering starting or improving your YouTube channel, remember that the script is not just important; it's the core ingredient that will set you on the path to YouTube stardom. While scripting alone won't guarantee success, it's the first and most essential step in creating content that stands out.

List-form Scripts

List-form videos offer a structured format for presenting information. Viewers appreciate the organized flow, knowing what to expect and how the content will be delivered. The segmented nature of lists can enhance viewer retention. Each item on the list represents a distinct point, making it easier for the audience to follow and remember. The videos are versatile and applicable across various niches. Whether it's technology, beauty, gaming, or education, the format can be adapted to suit diverse content categories. The Beauty of the list-form is that Lists create a sense of anticipation. As viewers progress through the countdown, they eagerly await the next item, fostering curiosity and keeping them engaged until the end. They are inherently shareable. Viewers are more likely to share content that is well-organized and provides value. Additionally, list-form videos often perform well in search results, contributing to discoverability.

Components of List-Form Scripts

Hooking the Audience: Begin with a compelling hook to grab the audience's attention. This can be a surprising fact, a thought-provoking question, or a teaser related to the list.

"Could this be the beginning of the world's greatest Mega project ever, or will the line become a trillion-dollar construction mistake that will eventually be abandoned? Let's find out."

Introduction to the List: Clearly introduce the theme or topic of the list. Outline what the audience can expect, emphasizing the value they will gain from watching the entire video.

Structured List Items: The Heart of the Script

Clarity and Consistency: Clearly state each list item, ensuring consistency in presentation. Whether it's a countdown or tips for improvement, maintain a clear and consistent structure.

Engaging Descriptions: Provide engaging and informative descriptions for each list item. Use storytelling techniques, anecdotes, or examples to enhance the viewer's understanding and connection.

Visual Support: Complement each list item with visual support. This could include images, graphics, or video clips that emphasize or illustrate the points being discussed.

Smooth Transitions: Guiding the Flow

Transition Phrases: Use transition phrases to smoothly move from one list item to the next. This helps maintain a cohesive flow and prevents the video from feeling disjointed.

Connective Narratives: Consider incorporating connective narratives between list items. These narratives can tie the entire list together, creating a seamless viewing experience.

Audience Engagement: Encouraging Interaction

Calls to Action (CTAs): Strategically place calls to action throughout the script. Encourage viewers to like, comment, share, and subscribe. Leverage engagement to boost the video's performance.

Interactive Elements: Introduce interactive elements, such as polls or quizzes related to the list. This not only engages the audience but also encourages participation and feedback.

Script Writing Guide for Informative and Speculative videos and Documentaries

Hook: Start with a captivating statement or question or two questions.
  - Tip: Use rhetorical questions or surprising facts to glue the viewer to watching the video.

Body: Feel free to use chapters if you think it fits the video. People tend to like it more with chapters and you could animate them as well.

Background Information: In this section, you lay the foundation for your audience to understand the subject matter.

Historical Context: Provide a timeline of key events that led to the current situation.

  - **Example:** "Sustainability wasn't always a buzzword. In the 1970s, the first Earth Day was celebrated, marking the beginning of the modern environmental movement."

Key Players: Introduce the organizations, governments, or individuals who have played a significant role in the issue.

- **Example:** "Organizations like Greenpeace and the WWF have been at the forefront of sustainability efforts."

Terminology: Define any jargon or specialized terms that the audience needs to understand.

- **Example:** "Before we delve deeper, let's understand what 'carbon footprint' really means."

Current Landscape: Describe the status quo, including any prevailing attitudes or misconceptions.

- **Example:** "Many people still believe that sustainability is just a trend, not realizing its long-term impact."

Section 2: Current Status

This section is where you update the audience on what's happening now.

Recent Developments: Discuss any new laws, technologies, or initiatives.

- **Example:** "Just last year, the European Union committed to becoming carbon neutral by 2050."

Case Studies: Use real-world examples to illustrate points.

- **Example:** "Let's take a look at Denmark, a country that produces more than half of its electricity from renewable sources."

Evidence: Support your points with data, quotes, or footage.

- **Example:** "According to a recent study, the project could..."

Section 3: Speculation

This section allows you to explore what might happen in the future.

Potential Outcomes: Discuss various scenarios, both optimistic and pessimistic.

- **Example:** "If current trends continue, we could see a 50% reduction in carbon emissions by 2030. But what if they don't?"

Challenges and Obstacles: Identify any hurdles that must be overcome.

- **Example:** "One major obstacle is political will. Without it, even the best-laid plans can falter."

Calls to Action: Suggest what needs to be done to achieve the best possible outcomes.

- **Example:** "It's not too late to turn things around, but it will require concerted effort from all sectors of society."

Section 4: Counterarguments and Rebuttals

Present Opposition: Share the views of those who disagree with the prevailing sentiment on the issue.

- **Example:** "Not everyone is on board with the sustainability movement. Some argue that it hampers economic growth."

Rebuttal: Offer evidence or arguments that counter these opposing views.

- **Example:** "However, studies have shown that sustainable practices can actually boost economic performance in the long run."

Section 5: Human Element

Personal Stories: Share anecdotes or personal stories that humanize the issue.

- **Example:** "Meet Emily, a farmer who switched to sustainable agriculture and saw her yields double."

Section 6: Global Impact

Wider Relevance: Explain how the issue affects the world at large, or different communities and ecosystems.

- **Example:** "The melting polar ice caps don't just affect polar bears; they have a ripple effect on weather patterns globally."

Section 7: Conclusion

Summary: Recap the main points.

Final Thoughts: Share a thought-provoking question or opinion.

- **Example:** "So, is this the future we've been waiting for?"

  Ask the viewer to share their opinion in the comments below

Cliffhanger: Use a cliffhanger to lead the viewer to watching the next video that appears on the screen at the end of the video. Feel free to suggest one of the videos on your channel to display at the end for this purpose.

Script Tone and Style

In the context of writing scripts for YouTube, "tone" and "style" refer to two distinct but interconnected aspects that contribute to the overall communication and presentation of content. Tone in writing refers to the author's attitude or emotional expression towards the subject matter. It encompasses the mood, feelings, and overall demeanor conveyed through the choice of words, sentence structures, and language. Tone is a powerful tool for setting the emotional atmosphere of the content and influencing how the audience perceives the information. In YouTube scripts, tone plays a crucial role in shaping the creator's on-screen persona and the overall mood of the content. The tone can range from formal and informative to casual and conversational, depending on the content's nature and the audience's expectations.

Style in writing refers to the unique manner in which an author expresses ideas, conveys information, and crafts sentences. It encompasses the author's individual voice, word choices, sentence structures, and overall approach to storytelling. Style is what makes a piece of writing distinctive and recognizable. In the context of YouTube scripts, style is the creator's signature way of presenting content. It involves aspects such as pacing, humor, storytelling techniques, and the overall aesthetic of the video. A consistent style helps in building a brand identity and fostering a connection with the audience.

While tone sets the emotional tone of the content, style is the vehicle through which that tone is expressed. For instance, a serious tone can be conveyed through a calm and measured style, while an enthusiastic tone may be expressed through a lively and energetic style. The choice of tone and style should align with the content's purpose and the preferences of the target audience. Adapting these elements ensures effective communication and audience engagement. Maintaining consistency in tone and style across videos contributes to a cohesive brand identity. Viewers may come to expect a certain tone and style from a specific creator, creating a sense of familiarity.

The overall tone of a documentary can significantly influence how the audience perceives and engages with the content. Here are some tones commonly used in documentaries, along with when and why you might choose them:

Informative

- **Use When:** The primary goal is to educate the audience.
- **Why:** An informative tone helps convey facts clearly and authoritatively.
- **Example:** "According to the Intergovernmental Panel on Climate Change, global temperatures could rise by 1.5°C as early as 2030. This documentary aims to provide a comprehensive overview of the science behind climate change."

Inspirational

- **Use When:** You want to motivate viewers to take action or change their perspective.
- **Why:** An inspirational tone can uplift the audience and encourage positive change.
- **Example:** "Meet the young activist who is taking the fight against climate change into his own hands. His story will inspire you to believe that change is possible."

Serious

- **Use When:** The subject matter is grave, sensitive, or requires a respectful approach.
- **Why:** A serious tone lends weight to the topic and underscores its importance.

Example: "The melting polar ice caps are not just a distant phenomenon; they are a dire warning of the catastrophic future that awaits us if immediate action is delayed."

Conversational

- **Use When:** You aim for a more relaxed, engaging style that invites viewers into a dialogue.
- **Why:** A conversational tone can make complex or challenging topics more accessible.
- **Example:** "So, you've probably heard that climate change is a big deal, right? But let's break down what that really means for you and me."

Dramatic

- **Use When:** You're telling a compelling story that involves conflict, suspense, or high emotional stakes.
- **Why:** A dramatic tone can heighten emotional investment and make the narrative more gripping.
- **Example:** "As wildfires rage and destructive hurricanes devastate communities, we are at a tipping point. The clock is ticking, and the planet's future hangs in the balance."

Humorous

- **Use When:** The subject matter allows for a lighter touch, and you want to entertain as well as inform.
- **Why:** Humor can make the documentary more enjoyable and help hold the audience's attention.
- **Example:** "Ever tried sunbathing in Antarctica? Well, if we don't do something about climate change, you might just be able to. Let's dive into the not-so-funny facts."

Critical

- **Use When:** You're examining flaws, failures, or injustices that need to be exposed.

- **Why:** A critical tone can provoke thought and encourage viewers to question the status quo.
- **Example:** "Despite overwhelming evidence, the federal government and corporations have failed to take adequate measures. This documentary exposes the negligence and greed that have accelerated climate change."

Optimistic

- **Use When:** You want to focus on positive aspects, solutions, or hopeful outcomes.
- **Why:** An optimistic tone can provide a counterbalance to grim or challenging topics and inspire hope.
- **Example:** "Innovation is leading the way. From replicable renewable energy to sustainable farming, we'll show you why there's hope for a greener future."

Nostalgic

- **Use When:** You're looking back at history, personal stories, or cultural phenomena.
- **Why:** A nostalgic tone can evoke emotional responses and make the past feel relevant to the present.
- **Example:** "Remember the winters when snow actually fell and summers weren't scorching? This documentary explores how climate has changed over the decades."

Neutral

- **Use When:** You aim to present facts without taking a stance, allowing viewers to form their own opinions.
- **Why:** A neutral tone can lend credibility and allow for a more balanced view of the subject matter.

- **Example:** "We present the facts and figures about climate change, along with perspectives from both sides of the debate, leaving you to form your own opinions."

Investigative

- **Use When:** You're uncovering new information, exposing wrongdoing, or diving deep into a complex issue.
- **Why:** An investigative tone adds an element of discovery and urgency to the documentary.
- **Example:** "We go undercover to expose the industries and individuals who are contributing the most to climate change, despite public claims of sustainability."

Empathetic

- **Use When:** You're dealing with human stories that require sensitivity and understanding.
- **Why:** An empathetic tone helps humanize the subjects and allows viewers to connect on an emotional level.
- **Example:** "Hear the heart-wrenching stories of families whose lives have been upended by climate disasters, and understand why this issue is a human one at its core."

In addition to these styles ensure that you plan for accompanying visuals, use SEO-friendly tags and descriptions, and encourage viewer interaction.

Mistakes to Avoid When Scripting for Your Channel

There is no excuse for ignorance these days as competition increases in the content creation niche. You can lose your audience by making any of these small but significant mistakes, the problem with making these mistakes is that the Youtube algorithm can be unforgiving, and if your video is suggested to the right audience but you made these blatant scripting mistakes, then you have lost the opportunity to acquire new subscribers. Let's take a look at a few scripting errors that can cost you tons of views.

1. **Mistake:** Excessive use of filler words like "um," "uh," "you know," and "like."

Why it Matters: Filler words can make the script sound less polished and distract viewers from the main content.

2. **Mistake:** Lack of a well-defined introduction, body, and conclusion.

Why it Matters: A clear structure helps viewers follow the narrative and understand the key points.

3. **Mistake:** Neglecting calls to action (CTAs) and interaction prompts.

Why it Matters: CTAs encourage engagement, such as likes, comments, and subscriptions, fostering a sense of community.

4. **Mistake:** Sudden shifts in tone or style throughout the script.

Why it Matters: Inconsistency can confuse the audience and disrupt the flow of the video.

5. **Mistake:** Incorporating industry-specific jargon without providing context or explanations.

Why it Matters: Viewers may feel alienated if they don't understand technical terms or specialized language.

6. **Mistake:** Relying heavily on clichés and overused expressions.

Why it Matters: Overused phrases can make the content sound generic and uninspired.

7. **Mistake:** Ignoring the importance of vivid and descriptive language.

Why it Matters: Engaging language helps create a mental image for the audience, enhancing their overall experience.

8. **Mistake:** Including excessive details that do not contribute to the main message.

Why it Matters: Overloading the script can overwhelm viewers and dilute the impact of the core content.

9. **Mistake:** Insensitivity to cultural nuances, language, or references.

Why it Matters: Content that lacks cultural awareness can alienate or offend certain audiences.

10. **Mistake:** Straying too far from natural speech patterns or sounding overly rehearsed.

Why it Matters: Artificial or overly rehearsed delivery can make the script feel robotic or insincere.

11. **Mistake:** Failing to tailor language and content to the preferences of the target audience.

Why it Matters: Content that doesn't resonate with the intended audience may struggle to capture attention.

12. **Mistake:** Delaying the delivery of engaging content or a compelling hook.

Why it Matters: Viewers may lose interest if the opening fails to capture their attention.

Script Writing for Watch Hours

Increasing watch hours on YouTube requires a strategic approach that goes beyond the conventional advice. To increase watch hours, you are basically buying your viewer's time with information. The question is, do you have the sort of information that can buy time, and can you deliver the information in a way that makes your audience stick around and possibly watch the next video? Here are a few things that you can do to rake in those watch hours that you need.

1. Create a narrative that unfolds across multiple videos, encouraging viewers to watch the entire series.
2. End each video with a compelling cliffhanger, prompting viewers to tune in for the next installment.
3. Craft a series of videos that collectively solve a mystery or puzzle, encouraging viewers to watch until the end for the big reveal.
4. Host live Q&A sessions where viewers can submit questions in advance, and each question becomes a separate segment in the video.
5. Break down a complex topic or challenge into a series of videos, with each video building upon the knowledge gained in the previous one.
6. Offer exclusive content or behind-the-scenes footage available only for a limited time, creating a sense of urgency.
7. Collaborate with other creators to curate themed playlists, linking your videos together.
8. Let your audience influence the content by incorporating their suggestions or challenges into your videos.
9. Document your progress on a particular project or skill over time, creating a sense of continuity.
10. Juggle multiple storylines or topics within a single video, appealing to a broader audience with varied interests.
11. Initiate challenges where viewers can participate virtually, with their entries featured in upcoming videos.
12. Develop a documentary-style series that takes viewers behind the scenes of your creative process.
13. Incorporate a series where you perform random acts of kindness based on viewers' suggestions.
14. Establish a consistent aesthetic or visual theme that spans across multiple videos, creating a recognizable series.

15. Create a series exploring hypothetical scenarios or alternative realities based on viewer suggestions.
16. Document personal or professional transformations over a series of videos, showcasing progress and growth. If you're a science channel, explore "what if" scenarios in physics or astronomy suggested by your audience.
17. Craft videos where viewers make choices that determine the direction of the content, enhancing interactivity. In a storytelling video, present options at critical points, and viewers choose which path the narrative takes.

Incorporating these unconventional ideas into your YouTube script not only increases watch hours but also fosters a unique and engaging viewing experience. Remember to stay authentic to your brand and audience while experimenting with these strategies to discover what resonates best with your viewers.

Script Writing for Subscribers

Getting people to watch your videos is one thing, getting them to subscribe to your channel is a totally different thing. Often time, when you see a video with as much as a million views, you can bet that the actual subscribers to the channel may be as few as tens of thousands. So, yes, it's way more challenging to get people to subscribe to your channel. But over time, some creators have used certain methods that have been really effective in growing their subscriber list. Here are some ideas and strategies that big channels have used over the years to garner massive subscribers to their channels:

1. Promise exclusive content or early access to subscribers, creating a sense of privilege.
2. Engage with your audience through interactive challenges or contests, encouraging them to subscribe for participation.
3. Conduct giveaways exclusively for subscribers, but keep the details a mystery until they hit subscribe.
4. Incorporate regular subscriber shoutouts or features in your videos to highlight community members.
5. Host live Q&A sessions where you specifically address questions from subscribers. For instance, Invite subscribers to submit questions before the video, making them feel involved in the content.
6. Celebrate subscriber milestones by creating personalized content or messages for your audience.
7. Initiate challenges or collaborations that involve your subscribers, fostering a sense of community.
8. Offer exclusive behind-the-scenes access for subscribers, providing glimpses of your creative process. Share snippets of your video-making process, showcasing the effort that goes into creating content.
9. Conduct polls allowing subscribers to influence future content decisions or topics.
10. Arrange virtual hangouts or meetups exclusively for subscribers, fostering a stronger connection.
11. Invite subscribers to share their stories or experiences, featuring them in your videos. Dedicate a segment to

narrating interesting stories submitted by subscribers, giving them a platform.

12. Propose challenges tied to achieving specific channel goals, encouraging viewers to subscribe for progress updates. Set a subscriber goal and promise to undertake a unique challenge when the milestone is reached.

13. Offer tutorials or content based on requests from subscribers, addressing their specific interests. Dedicate episodes to tutorials or guides requested by subscribers, showcasing their influence on your content.

14. Shine a spotlight on individual subscribers or their achievements in your videos. Feature a "Subscriber of the Month" segment, highlighting a subscriber's accomplishments or contributions.

15. Let subscribers choose challenges or activities for you to undertake in your videos. Run a series where subscribers suggest and vote on challenges for you to attempt, creating a dynamic and engaging interaction.

16. Design and release exclusive merchandise available only to subscribers, creating a sense of belonging. Introduce limited-edition merchandise or discounts that are accessible solely to your subscriber base.

17. Introduce a virtual pet adoption series where subscribers suggest names or characteristics for your "adopted" pet. Feature subscriber-suggested names and stories for your virtual pet in each episode, making it a collaborative and entertaining experience

18. Launch interactive challenges where subscribers participate for a chance to win exclusive prizes. Initiate a monthly challenge where subscribers submit creative content related to your niche, with the best entries receiving personalized shoutouts or prizes.

Making Money with Short Attention Spans

As attention spans shrink in the digital age, understanding how to effectively capture and retain viewer attention on YouTube becomes critical. Moreover, transforming those fleeting views into sustainable revenue streams requires a strategic approach that aligns with the unique characteristics of the platform. With an abundance of content vying for attention, viewers are quick to scroll, click away, or move on to the next video if they are not immediately captivated. According to studies, the average attention span on digital platforms is around 8 seconds, emphasizing the need for content creators to make a swift and compelling impact. While short attention spans pose a challenge, they also create opportunities for creators to craft engaging content that captures attention within those crucial initial seconds. YouTube's algorithm rewards videos that not only attract clicks but also keep viewers engaged for a significant duration.

Short attention spans are often associated with mobile viewing habits. YouTube Shorts caters the mobile-first audience, offering content creators a direct route to engage users who prefer consuming content on the go. YouTube

Shorts is designed for vertical video content, aligning with the prevalent trend of mobile device usage. With a large portion of viewers accessing content on smartphones, the vertical format ensures optimal viewing without the need to rotate screens. YouTube's algorithm heavily promotes Shorts, providing creators with increased visibility. The platform's recommendation system pushes Shorts to users who are more likely to engage with the format, resulting in a potentially broader audience reach.

YouTube Shorts opens up new avenues for creators to monetize their content. While the Shorts Fund provides an initial source of income based on views, the format's integration with traditional YouTube monetization models, such as ads and channel memberships, enhances revenue streams. Shorts foster community engagement through quick and shareable content. Users are more likely to interact with Shorts, leading to increased likes, shares, and comments, which, in turn, contribute to enhanced visibility and potential revenue.

Key Elements of Successful YouTube Shorts

The first few seconds are critical. Successful Shorts capture attention immediately. Begin with a compelling hook, ensuring viewers are intrigued from the start. Shorts thrive on brevity. Keep content concise and to the point. Focus on a single idea, joke, or message, avoiding unnecessary filler to maintain audience interest.

YouTube Shorts allows for experimentation. Try different formats, styles, and themes to identify what resonates best with your audience. Learn from the performance of each Short and iterate accordingly.

The Contrarian Script

Crafting a contrarian script requires a delicate balance between defying conventions and maintaining a cohesive, engaging narrative. By identifying the norms you wish to challenge, defining a clear message, and experimenting with various elements, you can create a script that not only breaks away from the ordinary but also resonates with audiences in a profound and memorable way. Remember, the power of a contrarian script lies not just in its divergence from conventions but in its ability to provoke thought, inspire discussion, and leave a lasting impact on those who experience it.

Remember the book "The Subtle Art of Not Giving A F*ck" The book became a huge hit because it twisted the arm of conventions, captivated audiences with its no-filter language, and sparked conversations that many were excited to have. A contrarian script is so powerful that it can create a huge upward spike in your views and subscriptions. So, the question is, how do you craft a contrarian script that automatically captures the attention of both target and non-target audience? Let's look at a few solid points:

1. Identify Conventions

Understanding the Norms: Before you can break the rules, you need to know what they are. Identify common themes, narrative structures, and tropes prevalent in the genre or niche you're exploring.

2. Define Your Message

Clarity of Purpose: Know what you want to convey through your script. Whether it's a commentary on societal norms, a satire, or a fresh perspective on a familiar theme, a clear message is the backbone of a contrarian script.

3. Challenge Assumptions

Question Everything: A contrarian script thrives on challenging assumptions. Question widely accepted beliefs or narrative patterns, forcing the audience to reconsider their perspectives.

4. Subvert Expectations

Plot Twists and Turns: Subvert audience expectations by introducing unexpected plot twists, unconventional character arcs, or narrative decisions. Keep viewers guessing and engaged with the unpredictability.

5. Character Complexity

Multi-dimensional Characters: Create characters that defy stereotypes. Avoid one-dimensional portrayals and research the complexities of human nature. This adds depth to your script and challenges audience preconceptions.

6. Play with Genre

Genre Blending: Experiment with genre conventions. Blend elements from different genres to create a unique and unexpected viewing experience. The collision of genres can generate intriguing outcomes.

7. Unconventional Structure

Narrative Experimentation: Break away from traditional narrative structures. Consider non-linear storytelling, fragmented timelines, or multiple perspectives to keep the audience engaged and intrigued.

8. Rethink Dialogue

Subtle and Nuanced: Challenge conventional dialogue patterns. Embrace subtlety and nuance in conversations, allowing characters to express themselves in ways that defy typical scriptwriting norms.

9. Explore Taboos

Tackle Taboo Subjects: Addressing taboo subjects can be a powerful way to create a contrarian script. Approach sensitive topics with sensitivity, aiming to provoke thought rather than simply shock.

10. Unorthodox Endings

Defy Resolution Expectations: Experiment with the resolution of your story. Conventional scripts often follow a formulaic path to resolution. Consider an open ending, an ambiguous conclusion, or a resolution that challenges expectations.

11. Visual Innovation

Visual Storytelling: Use visual elements to enhance the contrarian nature of your script. Experiment with unconventional cinematography, visual metaphors, or symbolic imagery that adds layers of meaning.

12. Symbolism and Allegory

Hidden Meanings: Incorporate symbolism and allegory into your script. Layers of hidden meanings can add depth to the narrative and encourage viewers to analyze and interpret the story on multiple levels.

13. Embrace Absurdity

Absurdist Elements: Inject elements of absurdity into your script. Embrace the irrational and the surreal, challenging the viewer's sense of reality in a way that is both thought-provoking and entertaining.

14. Social Commentary

Satirical Exploration: Use satire and humor to provide social commentary. A contrarian script can effectively critique societal norms and behaviors through humor, making the message more palatable.

While being contrarian can take you very far, there are also rules to this thing. The wrong statement, idea, or choice of words can also make you lose everything. You see, Youtube has standard guidelines and basically lines that content creators are not permitted to cross in their quest to provide information and entertainment. Let's take a look at what can get you blackballed in youtube.

Getting Demonetized Over Words?

YouTube thrives on creativity and expression. However, the landscape comes with its challenges, one of the most significant being the risk of demonetization. While YouTube encourages free speech, certain words, phrases, ideologies, or content can potentially lead to demonetization, blacklisting, or even channel suspension. Understanding the words and content that can pose risks will provide insights on how much freedom content creators actually have, especially when it comes to scripting.

Firstly, Youtube is a business, so it maintains advertiser-friendly guidelines to ensure that ads appear on content suitable for a broad audience. Violating these guidelines can lead to demonetization. It employs a combination of automated systems and human reviewers to assess content. The automated system flags potential issues, and human reviewers provide context and make nuanced decisions.

Words, Phrases, and Ideologies at Risk:

1. Hate Speech and Discrimination

Any content that promotes hate speech based on attributes such as race, ethnicity, gender, religion, disability, or sexual orientation is a red flag. Creators must avoid using derogatory terms or promoting discriminatory ideologies.

2. Violence and Harm

Content that glorifies or incites violence, harm, or dangerous activities is likely to be demonetized. Creators should steer clear of scripting content that encourages harmful behavior.

3. Controversial Topics

While creators have the right to discuss controversial topics, presenting them in a sensationalized or inappropriate manner can lead to demonetization. Proper contextualization and sensitivity are crucial.

4. Explicit Language and Adult Content

Overuse of explicit language, sexual content, or graphic imagery can trigger demonetization. Creators should be mindful of their language and visuals, especially in the first moments of a video.

5. Misinformation and Conspiracy Theories

YouTube takes a strong stance against content that spreads misinformation or promotes conspiracy theories. Creators should fact-check information before including it in their scripts to avoid demonetization.

6. Harassment and Bullying

Content that harasses or bullies individuals or groups is against YouTube's guidelines. Creators must avoid scripting content that fosters a hostile environment.

7. Sensitive Events and Tragedies

Insensitive Handling of Sensitive Events: Scripting content that exploits or makes light of sensitive events, tragedies, or disasters can result in demonetization. Creators should approach such topics with care and empathy.

8. Drugs and Dangerous Substances

Content that promotes or glorifies the use of drugs or dangerous substances is not ad-friendly. Creators must be cautious about scripting content that showcases or endorses substance abuse.

Remember, creativity can thrive within the bounds of responsibility, and a well-crafted script can spark meaningful conversations without compromising the sustainability of your channel.

Evergreen Content Vs. New Trends

While evergreen content ensures longevity and sustained relevance, embracing trends can bring immediate visibility and audience engagement. Evergreen content stands the test of time. It remains relevant to viewers regardless of when it's consumed, offering value beyond current trends or time-sensitive events. It focuses on topics that have enduring appeal. Educational content, how-to guides, and fundamental concepts within a niche are typical examples. Evergreen videos generate consistent views over an extended period. They become foundational pieces of a channel, attracting new viewers and maintaining a steady flow of traffic. This form of content also benefits from strategic keyword optimization. Use keywords with enduring relevance to ensure your video remains discoverable. The Creator could also repurpose evergreen content across different platforms to maximize its reach. Blogs, podcasts, or social media snippets can extend the life of the content. So, how does this compare to trending contents?

Trending topics are subjects that are currently popular or widely discussed. They have the potential to generate rapid views and engagement. Creating content around trending topics allows you to ride the wave of current interest. This can result in increased visibility and subscriber growth. Videos centered on trending topics can experience rapid increases in views, especially during the peak of the trend. This can contribute to short-term success. Scripting for trending topics requires a quick turnaround. Be agile in your scripting process to capitalize on the immediacy of the trend.

The question is, how does a creator balance both forms or leverage them to build a profitable channel? You can Diversify your content by blending evergreen pieces with trend-responsive videos. This maintains a steady flow of long-term views while capitalizing on immediate trends. Plan your content calendar strategically. Allocate slots for evergreen content to maintain consistent traffic and reserve slots for trending topics to capture immediate interest. Develop an adaptable scripting style that allows for quick turnarounds when scripting for trending topics. Be agile in your approach to stay responsive to current discussions. However, be selective about the trends you chase. Not every trend will align with your channel's identity, so choose those that resonate with your audience.

More Books from the Author

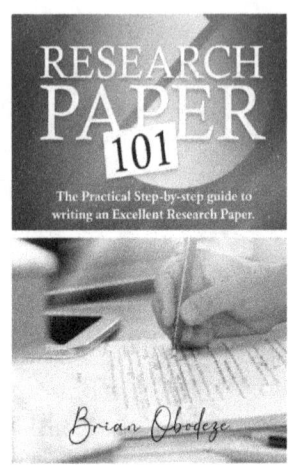

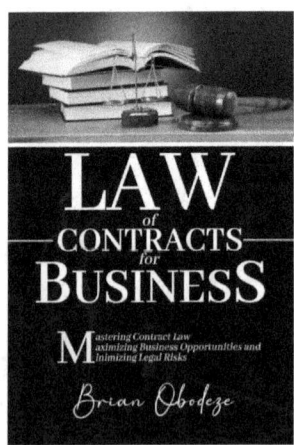

Available on Amazon KDP